AF450146

THIS NOTEBOOK BELONGS TO:

Website:
User Name:
Password:
Notes:

Website:
User Name:
Password:
Notes:

Website:
User Name:
Password:
Notes:

Website:
User Name:
Password:
Notes:

Website:
User Name:
Password:
Notes:

Website:
User Name:
Password:
Notes:

Website:
User Name:
Password:
Notes:

Website:
User Name:
Password:
Notes:

Website:
User Name:
Password:
Notes:

Website:
User Name:
Password:
Notes:

Website:
User Name:
Password:
Notes:

Website:
User Name:
Password:
Notes:

Website:
User Name:
Password:
Notes:

Website:
User Name:
Password:
Notes:

Website:
User Name:
Password:
Notes:

Website:
User Name:
Password:
Notes:

Website:
User Name:
Password:
Notes:

Website:
User Name:
Password:
Notes:

Website:
User Name:
Password:
Notes:

Website:
User Name:
Password:
Notes:

Website:
User Name:
Password:
Notes:

Website:
User Name:
Password:
Notes:

Website:
User Name:
Password:
Notes:

Website:
User Name:
Password:
Notes:

Website:
User Name:
Password:
Notes:

Website:
User Name:
Password:
Notes:

Website:
User Name:
Password:
Notes:

Website:
User Name:
Password:
Notes:

Website:
User Name:
Password:
Notes:

Website:
User Name:
Password:
Notes:

Website:
User Name:
Password:
Notes:

Website:
User Name:
Password:
Notes:

Website:
User Name:
Password:
Notes:

Website:
User Name:
Password:
Notes:

Website:
User Name:
Password:
Notes:

Website:
User Name:
Password:
Notes:

Website:
User Name:
Password:
Notes:

Website:
User Name:
Password:
Notes:

Website:
User Name:
Password:
Notes:

Website:
User Name:
Password:
Notes:

Website:
User Name:
Password:
Notes:

Website:
User Name:
Password:
Notes:

Website:
User Name:
Password:
Notes:

Website:
User Name:
Password:
Notes:

Website:
User Name:
Password:
Notes:

C

C

Website:
User Name:
Password:
Notes:

Website:
User Name:
Password:
Notes:

Website:
User Name:
Password:
Notes:

Website:
User Name:
Password:
Notes:

Website:
User Name:
Password:
Notes:

Website:
User Name:
Password:
Notes:

Website:
User Name:
Password:
Notes:

Website:
User Name:
Password:
Notes:

Website:
User Name:
Password:
Notes:

Website:
User Name:
Password:
Notes:

Website:
User Name:
Password:
Notes:

Website:
User Name:
Password:
Notes:

Website:
User Name:
Password:
Notes:

Website:
User Name:
Password:
Notes:

Website:
User Name:
Password:
Notes:

Website:
User Name:
Password:
Notes:

Website:
User Name:
Password:
Notes:

Website:
User Name:
Password:
Notes:

Website:
User Name:
Password:
Notes:

Website:
User Name:
Password:
Notes:

D

D

Website:
User Name:
Password:
Notes:

Website:
User Name:
Password:
Notes:

Website:
User Name:
Password:
Notes:

Website:
User Name:
Password:
Notes:

Website:
User Name:
Password:
Notes:

Website:
User Name:
Password:
Notes:

Website:
User Name:
Password:
Notes:

Website:
User Name:
Password:
Notes:

Website:
User Name:
Password:
Notes:

Website:
User Name:
Password:
Notes:

D

D

Website:
User Name:
Password:
Notes:

Website:
User Name:
Password:
Notes:

Website:
User Name:
Password:
Notes:

Website:
User Name:
Password:
Notes:

Website:
User Name:
Password:
Notes:

Website:
User Name:
Password:
Notes:

Website:
User Name:
Password:
Notes:

Website:
User Name:
Password:
Notes:

Website:
User Name:
Password:
Notes:

Website:
User Name:
Password:
Notes:

Website:
User Name:
Password:
Notes:

E

Website:
User Name:
Password:
Notes:

Website:
User Name:
Password:
Notes:

Website:
User Name:
Password:
Notes:

Website:
User Name:
Password:
Notes:

Website:
User Name:
Password:
Notes:

Website:
User Name:
Password:
Notes:

Website:
User Name:
Password:
Notes:

Website:
User Name:
Password:
Notes:

Website:
User Name:
Password:
Notes:

Website:	
User Name:	
Password:	
Notes:	

Website:	
User Name:	
Password:	
Notes:	

Website:	
User Name:	
Password:	
Notes:	

Website:	
User Name:	
Password:	
Notes:	

Website:	
User Name:	
Password:	
Notes:	

Website:
User Name:
Password:
Notes:

Website:
User Name:
Password:
Notes:

Website:
User Name:
Password:
Notes:

Website:
User Name:
Password:
Notes:

Website:
User Name:
Password:
Notes:

Website:
User Name:
Password:
Notes:

Website:
User Name:
Password:
Notes:

Website:
User Name:
Password:
Notes:

Website:
User Name:
Password:
Notes:

Website:
User Name:
Password:
Notes:

Website:
User Name:
Password:
Notes:

Website:
User Name:
Password:
Notes:

Website:
User Name:
Password:
Notes:

Website:
User Name:
Password:
Notes:

Website:
User Name:
Password:
Notes:

F

Website:
User Name:
Password:
Notes:

Website:
User Name:
Password:
Notes:

Website:
User Name:
Password:
Notes:

Website:
User Name:
Password:
Notes:

Website:
User Name:
Password:
Notes:

Website:
User Name:
Password:
Notes:

Website:
User Name:
Password:
Notes:

Website:
User Name:
Password:
Notes:

Website:
User Name:
Password:
Notes:

Website:
User Name:
Password:
Notes:

Website: ____________________
User Name: ____________________
Password: ____________________
Notes: ____________________
____

Website: ____________________
User Name: ____________________
Password: ____________________
Notes: ____________________
____

Website: ____________________
User Name: ____________________
Password: ____________________
Notes: ____________________
____

Website: ____________________
User Name: ____________________
Password: ____________________
Notes: ____________________
____

Website: ____________________
User Name: ____________________
Password: ____________________
Notes: ____________________
____

Website:
User Name:
Password:
Notes:

Website:
User Name:
Password:
Notes:

Website:
User Name:
Password:
Notes:

Website:
User Name:
Password:
Notes:

Website:
User Name:
Password:
Notes:

Website:
User Name:
Password:
Notes:

Website:
User Name:
Password:
Notes:

Website:
User Name:
Password:
Notes:

Website:
User Name:
Password:
Notes:

Website:
User Name:
Password:
Notes:

Website: ______________________________
User Name: ______________________________
Password: ______________________________
Notes: ______________________________

____

Website: ______________________________
User Name: ______________________________
Password: ______________________________
Notes: ______________________________

____

Website: ______________________________
User Name: ______________________________
Password: ______________________________
Notes: ______________________________

____

Website: ______________________________
User Name: ______________________________
Password: ______________________________
Notes: ______________________________

____

Website: ______________________________
User Name: ______________________________
Password: ______________________________
Notes: ______________________________

____

Website:
User Name:
Password:
Notes:

Website:
User Name:
Password:
Notes:

Website:
User Name:
Password:
Notes:

Website:
User Name:
Password:
Notes:

Website:
User Name:
Password:
Notes:

Website:
User Name:
Password:
Notes:

Website:
User Name:
Password:
Notes:

Website:
User Name:
Password:
Notes:

Website:
User Name:
Password:
Notes:

Website:
User Name:
Password:
Notes:

Website:
User Name:
Password:
Notes:

Website:
User Name:
Password:
Notes:

Website:
User Name:
Password:
Notes:

Website:
User Name:
Password:
Notes:

Website:
User Name:
Password:
Notes:

Website:
User Name:
Password:
Notes:

Website:
User Name:
Password:
Notes:

Website:
User Name:
Password:
Notes:

Website:
User Name:
Password:
Notes:

Website:
User Name:
Password:
Notes:

Website:
User Name:
Password:
Notes:

Website:
User Name:
Password:
Notes:

Website:
User Name:
Password:
Notes:

Website:
User Name:
Password:
Notes:

Website:
User Name:
Password:
Notes:

Website: ____________________________
User Name: ____________________________
Password: ____________________________
Notes: ____________________________

____

Website: ____________________________
User Name: ____________________________
Password: ____________________________
Notes: ____________________________

____

Website: ____________________________
User Name: ____________________________
Password: ____________________________
Notes: ____________________________

____

Website: ____________________________
User Name: ____________________________
Password: ____________________________
Notes: ____________________________

____

Website: ____________________________
User Name: ____________________________
Password: ____________________________
Notes: ____________________________

____

Website:
User Name:
Password:
Notes:

Website:
User Name:
Password:
Notes:

Website:
User Name:
Password:
Notes:

Website:
User Name:
Password:
Notes:

Website:
User Name:
Password:
Notes:

Website:
User Name:
Password:
Notes:

Website:
User Name:
Password:
Notes:

Website:
User Name:
Password:
Notes:

Website:
User Name:
Password:
Notes:

Website:
User Name:
Password:
Notes:

Website:
User Name:
Password:
Notes:

Website:
User Name:
Password:
Notes:

Website:
User Name:
Password:
Notes:

Website:
User Name:
Password:
Notes:

Website:
User Name:
Password:
Notes:

Website:
User Name:
Password:
Notes:

Website:
User Name:
Password:
Notes:

Website:
User Name:
Password:
Notes:

Website:
User Name:
Password:
Notes:

Website:
User Name:
Password:
Notes:

Website:
User Name:
Password:
Notes:

Website:
User Name:
Password:
Notes:

Website:
User Name:
Password:
Notes:

Website:
User Name:
Password:
Notes:

Website:
User Name:
Password:
Notes:

Website:
User Name:
Password:
Notes:

Website:
User Name:
Password:
Notes:

Website:
User Name:
Password:
Notes:

Website:
User Name:
Password:
Notes:

Website:
User Name:
Password:
Notes:

Website:
User Name:
Password:
Notes:

Website:
User Name:
Password:
Notes:

Website:
User Name:
Password:
Notes:

Website:
User Name:
Password:
Notes:

Website:
User Name:
Password:
Notes:

Website:
User Name:
Password:
Notes:

Website:
User Name:
Password:
Notes:

Website:
User Name:
Password:
Notes:

Website:
User Name:
Password:
Notes:

Website:
User Name:
Password:
Notes:

Website:
User Name:
Password:
Notes:

Website:
User Name:
Password:
Notes:

Website:
User Name:
Password:
Notes:

Website:
User Name:
Password:
Notes:

Website:
User Name:
Password:
Notes:

Website:
User Name:
Password:
Notes:

Website:
User Name:
Password:
Notes:

Website:
User Name:
Password:
Notes:

Website:
User Name:
Password:
Notes:

Website:
User Name:
Password:
Notes:

L

Website:
User Name:
Password:
Notes:

Website:
User Name:
Password:
Notes:

Website:
User Name:
Password:
Notes:

Website:
User Name:
Password:
Notes:

Website:
User Name:
Password:
Notes:

Website:

User Name:

Password:

Notes:

Website:

User Name:

Password:

Notes:

Website:

User Name:

Password:

Notes:

Website:

User Name:

Password:

Notes:

Website:

User Name:

Password:

Notes:

Website:
User Name:
Password:
Notes:

Website:
User Name:
Password:
Notes:

Website:
User Name:
Password:
Notes:

Website:
User Name:
Password:
Notes:

Website:
User Name:
Password:
Notes:

Website:
User Name:
Password:
Notes:

Website:
User Name:
Password:
Notes:

Website:
User Name:
Password:
Notes:

Website:
User Name:
Password:
Notes:

Website:
User Name:
Password:
Notes:

M

Website:
User Name:
Password:
Notes:

Website:
User Name:
Password:
Notes:

Website:
User Name:
Password:
Notes:

Website:
User Name:
Password:
Notes:

Website:
User Name:
Password:
Notes:

Website:
User Name:
Password:
Notes:

Website:
User Name:
Password:
Notes:

Website:
User Name:
Password:
Notes:

M

Website:
User Name:
Password:
Notes:

Website:
User Name:
Password:
Notes:

Website:
User Name:
Password:
Notes:

Website:
User Name:
Password:
Notes:

Website:
User Name:
Password:
Notes:

Website:
User Name:
Password:
Notes:

Website:
User Name:
Password:
Notes:

M

Website:
User Name:
Password:
Notes:

Website:
User Name:
Password:
Notes:

Website:
User Name:
Password:
Notes:

Website:
User Name:
Password:
Notes:

Website:
User Name:
Password:
Notes:

Website:
User Name:
Password:
Notes:

Website:
User Name:
Password:
Notes:

Website:
User Name:
Password:
Notes:

Website:
User Name:
Password:
Notes:

Website:
User Name:
Password:
Notes:

N

Website:
User Name:
Password:
Notes:

Website:
User Name:
Password:
Notes:

Website:
User Name:
Password:
Notes:

Website:
User Name:
Password:
Notes:

Website:
User Name:
Password:
Notes:

Website:
User Name:
Password:
Notes:

Website:
User Name:
Password:
Notes:

Website:
User Name:
Password:
Notes:

Website:
User Name:
Password:
Notes:

Website:
User Name:
Password:
Notes:

Website:
User Name:
Password:
Notes:

Website:
User Name:
Password:
Notes:

Website:
User Name:
Password:
Notes:

Website:
User Name:
Password:
Notes:

Website:
User Name:
Password:
Notes:

Website:
User Name:
Password:
Notes:

Website:
User Name:
Password:
Notes:

Website:
User Name:
Password:
Notes:

Website:
User Name:
Password:
Notes:

Website:
User Name:
Password:
Notes:

Website:
User Name:
Password:
Notes:

Website:
User Name:
Password:
Notes:

Website:
User Name:
Password:
Notes:

Website:
User Name:
Password:
Notes:

Website:
User Name:
Password:
Notes:

Website:
User Name:
Password:
Notes:

Website:
User Name:
Password:
Notes:

O

Website:
User Name:
Password:
Notes:

Website:
User Name:
Password:
Notes:

Website:
User Name:
Password:
Notes:

Website:
User Name:
Password:
Notes:

Website:
User Name:
Password:
Notes:

Website:
User Name:
Password:
Notes:

Website:
User Name:
Password:
Notes:

Website:
User Name:
Password:
Notes:

P

Website:
User Name:
Password:
Notes:

Website:
User Name:
Password:
Notes:

Website:
User Name:
Password:
Notes:

Website:
User Name:
Password:
Notes:

Website:
User Name:
Password:
Notes:

Website:
User Name:
Password:
Notes:

Website:
User Name:
Password:
Notes:

Website:
User Name:
Password:
Notes:

Website:
User Name:
Password:
Notes:

Website:
User Name:
Password:
Notes:

Website:
User Name:
Password:
Notes:

Website:
User Name:
Password:
Notes:

Website:
User Name:
Password:
Notes:

Website:
User Name:
Password:
Notes:

Website:
User Name:
Password:
Notes:

Website:
User Name:
Password:
Notes:

Website:
User Name:
Password:
Notes:

Website:
User Name:
Password:
Notes:

Website:
User Name:
Password:
Notes:

Website:
User Name:
Password:
Notes:

Website:
User Name:
Password:
Notes:

Website:
User Name:
Password:
Notes:

Website:
User Name:
Password:
Notes:

Website:
User Name:
Password:
Notes:

Website:
User Name:
Password:
Notes:

Website:
User Name:
Password:
Notes:

Website:
User Name:
Password:
Notes:

Website:
User Name:
Password:
Notes:

Website:
User Name:
Password:
Notes:

Website:
User Name:
Password:
Notes:

Website:
User Name:
Password:
Notes:

Website:
User Name:
Password:
Notes:

Website:
User Name:
Password:
Notes:

Website:
User Name:
Password:
Notes:

Website:
User Name:
Password:
Notes:

Website:
User Name:
Password:
Notes:

Website:
User Name:
Password:
Notes:

Website:
User Name:
Password:
Notes:

Website:
User Name:
Password:
Notes:

Website:
User Name:
Password:
Notes:

R

Website:
User Name:
Password:
Notes:

Website:
User Name:
Password:
Notes:

Website:
User Name:
Password:
Notes:

Website:
User Name:
Password:
Notes:

Website:
User Name:
Password:
Notes:

Website:
User Name:
Password:
Notes:

Website:
User Name:
Password:
Notes:

Website:
User Name:
Password:
Notes:

Website:
User Name:
Password:
Notes:

Website:
User Name:
Password:
Notes:

Website:
User Name:
Password:
Notes:

Website:
User Name:
Password:
Notes:

Website:
User Name:
Password:
Notes:

Website:
User Name:
Password:
Notes:

Website:
User Name:
Password:
Notes:

Website:
User Name:
Password:
Notes:

Website:
User Name:
Password:
Notes:

Website:
User Name:
Password:
Notes:

Website:
User Name:
Password:
Notes:

Website:
User Name:
Password:
Notes:

Website:
User Name:
Password:
Notes:

Website:
User Name:
Password:
Notes:

Website:
User Name:
Password:
Notes:

Website:
User Name:
Password:
Notes:

Website:
User Name:
Password:
Notes:

Website:
User Name:
Password:
Notes:

Website:
User Name:
Password:
Notes:

Website:
User Name:
Password:
Notes:

Website:
User Name:
Password:
Notes:

Website:
User Name:
Password:
Notes:

Website:
User Name:
Password:
Notes:

Website:
User Name:
Password:
Notes:

Website:
User Name:
Password:
Notes:

Website:
User Name:
Password:
Notes:

Website:
User Name:
Password:
Notes:

Website: ___________________
User Name: ___________________
Password: ___________________
Notes: ___________________

____

Website: ___________________
User Name: ___________________
Password: ___________________
Notes: ___________________

____

Website: ___________________
User Name: ___________________
Password: ___________________
Notes: ___________________

____

Website: ___________________
User Name: ___________________
Password: ___________________
Notes: ___________________

____

Website: ___________________
User Name: ___________________
Password: ___________________
Notes: ___________________

____

T

Website:
User Name:
Password:
Notes:

Website:
User Name:
Password:
Notes:

Website:
User Name:
Password:
Notes:

Website:
User Name:
Password:
Notes:

T

Website:
User Name:
Password:
Notes:

Website:
User Name:
Password:
Notes:

Website:
User Name:
Password:
Notes:

Website:
User Name:
Password:
Notes:

Website:
User Name:
Password:
Notes:

Website:
User Name:
Password:
Notes:

Website:
User Name:
Password:
Notes:

Website:
User Name:
Password:
Notes:

Website:
User Name:
Password:
Notes:

Website:
User Name:
Password:
Notes:

Website:
User Name:
Password:
Notes:

Website:
User Name:
Password:
Notes:

Website:
User Name:
Password:
Notes:

Website:
User Name:
Password:
Notes:

Website:
User Name:
Password:
Notes:

U

Website:
User Name:
Password:
Notes:

Website:

User Name:

Password:

Notes:

Website:

User Name:

Password:

Notes:

Website:

User Name:

Password:

Notes:

Website:

User Name:

Password:

Notes:

Website:

User Name:

Password:

Notes:

Website:
User Name:
Password:
Notes:

Website:
User Name:
Password:
Notes:

Website:
User Name:
Password:
Notes:

Website:
User Name:
Password:
Notes:

U

Website:
User Name:
Password:
Notes:

Website:
User Name:
Password:
Notes:

Website:
User Name:
Password:
Notes:

Website:
User Name:
Password:
Notes:

Website:
User Name:
Password:
Notes:

U

Website:
User Name:
Password:
Notes:

Website:
User Name:
Password:
Notes:

Website:
User Name:
Password:
Notes:

Website:
User Name:
Password:
Notes:

Website:
User Name:
Password:
Notes:

Website:
User Name:
Password:
Notes:

V

Website:
User Name:
Password:
Notes:

Website:
User Name:
Password:
Notes:

Website:
User Name:
Password:
Notes:

Website:
User Name:
Password:
Notes:

V

Website:
User Name:
Password:
Notes:

Website:
User Name:
Password:
Notes:

Website:
User Name:
Password:
Notes:

Website:
User Name:
Password:
Notes:

Website:
User Name:
Password:
Notes:

V

Website:
User Name:
Password:
Notes:

Website:
User Name:
Password:
Notes:

Website:
User Name:
Password:
Notes:

Website:
User Name:
Password:
Notes:

Website:
User Name:
Password:
Notes:

V

Website:
User Name:
Password:
Notes:

Website:
User Name:
Password:
Notes:

Website:
User Name:
Password:
Notes:

Website:
User Name:
Password:
Notes:

Website:
User Name:
Password:
Notes:

Website:
User Name:
Password:
Notes:

W

Website:
User Name:
Password:
Notes:

Website:
User Name:
Password:
Notes:

Website:
User Name:
Password:
Notes:

Website:
User Name:
Password:
Notes:

Website:
User Name:
Password:
Notes:

W

Website:
User Name:
Password:
Notes:

Website:
User Name:
Password:
Notes:

Website:
User Name:
Password:
Notes:

Website:
User Name:
Password:
Notes:

Website:
User Name:
Password:
Notes:

W

Website:
User Name:
Password:
Notes:

Website:
User Name:
Password:
Notes:

Website:
User Name:
Password:
Notes:

Website:
User Name:
Password:
Notes:

Website:
User Name:
Password:
Notes:

W

Website: _______________
User Name: _______________
Password: _______________
Notes: _______________

____

Website: _______________
User Name: _______________
Password: _______________
Notes: _______________

____

Website: _______________
User Name: _______________
Password: _______________
Notes: _______________

____

Website: _______________
User Name: _______________
Password: _______________
Notes: _______________

____

Website: _______________
User Name: _______________
Password: _______________
Notes: _______________

X

Website:

User Name:

Password:

Notes:

Website:

User Name:

Password:

Notes:

Website:

User Name:

Password:

Notes:

Website:

User Name:

Password:

Notes:

Website:

User Name:

Password:

Notes:

X

Website:
User Name:
Password:
Notes:

Website:
User Name:
Password:
Notes:

Website:
User Name:
Password:
Notes:

Website:
User Name:
Password:
Notes:

Website:
User Name:
Password:
Notes:

X

Website:

User Name:

Password:

Notes:

Website:

User Name:

Password:

Notes:

Website:

User Name:

Password:

Notes:

Website:

User Name:

Password:

Notes:

Website:

User Name:

Password:

Notes:

X

Website:
User Name:
Password:
Notes:

Website:
User Name:
Password:
Notes:

Website:
User Name:
Password:
Notes:

Website:
User Name:
Password:
Notes:

Website:
User Name:
Password:
Notes:

Y

Website: ___________________________
User Name: ___________________________
Password: ___________________________
Notes: ___________________________
____

Website: ___________________________
User Name: ___________________________
Password: ___________________________
Notes: ___________________________
____

Website: ___________________________
User Name: ___________________________
Password: ___________________________
Notes: ___________________________
____

Website: ___________________________
User Name: ___________________________
Password: ___________________________
Notes: ___________________________
____

Website: ___________________________
User Name: ___________________________
Password: ___________________________
Notes: ___________________________
____

Y

Website:
User Name:
Password:
Notes:

Website:
User Name:
Password:
Notes:

Website:
User Name:
Password:
Notes:

Website:
User Name:
Password:
Notes:

Website:
User Name:
Password:
Notes:

Y

Website:
User Name:
Password:
Notes:

Website:
User Name:
Password:
Notes:

Website:
User Name:
Password:
Notes:

Website:
User Name:
Password:
Notes:

Website:
User Name:
Password:
Notes:

Y

Website:
User Name:
Password:
Notes:

Website:
User Name:
Password:
Notes:

Website:
User Name:
Password:
Notes:

Website:
User Name:
Password:
Notes:

Website:
User Name:
Password:
Notes:

Z

Website:
User Name:
Password:
Notes:

Website:
User Name:
Password:
Notes:

Website:
User Name:
Password:
Notes:

Website:
User Name:
Password:
Notes:

Website:
User Name:
Password:
Notes:

Z

Website:
User Name:
Password:
Notes:

Website:
User Name:
Password:
Notes:

Website:
User Name:
Password:
Notes:

Website:
User Name:
Password:
Notes:

Website:
User Name:
Password:
Notes:

Z

Website:
User Name:
Password:
Notes:

Website:
User Name:
Password:
Notes:

Website:
User Name:
Password:
Notes:

Website:
User Name:
Password:
Notes:

Website:
User Name:
Password:
Notes:

Z